A KING AMONG MEN

There are many men but only one true king

Oyindamola Ogunbunmi

ISBN-13: 9798847748391
ISBN-10: 9798847748391

Cover design by: Peter's Media
Peter's Media's Number: +2348130826460
Printed in the Federal Republic Of Nigeria

This book is dedicated first to God almighty, who has made it possible to release this book and to every man who is very intentional about their growth and trying to be a better leader, father, husband, uncle and brother to their generation. To every man reading this book, I respect you. Yes, YOU ARE A KING AMONG, MEN!

CONTENTS

INTRODUCTION

There is a king in every man, but not everyone has been able to activate their kingship potential; you can call yourself a king but not have the qualities of a king.

How can you stand out in this generation and be admired by the actual queens, is a king defined by money or his latest car? I know society has limited a man to just chasing after material things, but I believe that acquiring things is not the only essence of life.

To be honoured and celebrated among men, you need to unplug what society has told you about being a man. Have you tried to question the old ideas ruled by our world today?

Should a man sleep with every lady before being considered a King?? Should a man get angry or have a stern face every time?? Does asking for help as a man makes you weak???
I won't neglect that God has made Every man a leader in his own home, but that calls for great responsibility! Is leadership portrayed the best way in our society today?? To be a good leader, you need to unlearn, relearn and learn.

I am writing this book because the menfolk have been neglected for too long; some of my male friends said they are always left to figure out life by themselves, so most men are shaped by ancient conventional knowledge of how society wants the man to be, and this isn't doing us all any good. Still, it is affecting the country; no wonder we have a lot of violence in our society today. Men are leaders, and their actions influence the country on a larger scale. We can never be better than the head that leads us.

In this book, you will find out precisely what makes a man a king in a queen's eye and, most of all, God; you can call yourself a king all day and not be considered one; what is the attitude of a king?? The mindset of a king?? Does a man become a king just by the amount he has in his bank account?? I added a bonus point on how to get the woman of your dreams?? How to approach a lady?? How to Guard your heart as a man?? I will reveal some secrets to you; it's more like I'm betraying the queens, but as long as it helps, let us find out. HAPPY READING, VIOLA!!!!

SUBMITTING

Someone influences us whether we like it or not; your belief system is made up of what you have been taught over the years since you are a child; as a man, you must submit to God in a Man; when God wants to lift a man he sends a man, without submission you can never know how to navigate through life there is a lot of men out here that beliefs they know it all, I believe every stage of our life needs mentoring, and if we refuse mentoring then we will have to go through a long process.

A mentor makes the journey faster since he has taken the same route. Submitting to authority makes you accountable; I *notice that our fathers' generation lived an authoritative life; they believe that being a man means they can do anything without being submitted to someone; the* word **" I am a man on my own"** is scary. You can't be a king when you haven't been mentored by one; before David became a king, he first was a shepherd before being promoted to the palace; there was a time of learning and reshaping.

Why did you do things on reflex every time? Just because you feel like it now doesn't mean that is how it should be. Raymond doesn't believe in submitting; He feels he can get away with any gruesome action. He talks anyhow, shouts at his family, and beats his sister; he wants everyone to be scared and fidget when they see him; he sees it as a sign of respect.

Many men are raised this way; they are taught this way because of the examples laid down by their fathers. Some men grew up to see their father beat their mother, shout at them; when dad is around, don't put on the TV, we always say, you saw how people run Helter Skelter by just hearing the sound of dads car and even if you don't like this as a man there is a higher chance of probability that you have seen it as normal to beat a woman. Did you know that 27.4% of abusers has a record of domestic violence? More reason you should submit to an authority that has succeeded in what your parents didn't succeed in.

There are two people you must submit to, *the first person is God, and the second person is someone that knows something that you don't know; I* notice that a lot of men work on their finances alone without working on other areas of life, there is a limit to where money can take you in life.

Still, it would be best to have good ethics and character to stand out. Therefore, you need some people in your life, whether friends, families e.t.c to help shape you into a good leader for your future family or family.

✓ Submitting to God

fish cannot survive without water; no man can survive without God. The reason why the male gender is never willing to surrender in situations is that society has said they have to lead every time, so in cases where they feel helpless. They choose to keep it to themselves and suffer in silence because a man is perceived as someone who shouldn't get hurt or cry during challenging times.

There is a limit to what you can do for yourself as a man; I have a friend who once told me he is looking for money now, he doesn't need God, but the truth is you need God regardless of the circumstances, in making a business transaction, in relating with the right people in your life, knowing what to do per time.

Submitting to God helps you choose the right spouse; you will be able to see. I have never seen a man who offers his entire life to God that doesn't succeed in life; devote your life to God!

✓ Submitting to someone who knows better

There is someone in your field that knows better than you; there is a bulk of knowledge you have about something that I don't have, Men are built to compete, but there are situations you need to be a learner and a good student.

No man is an island; you can't know it all; even in marriage, there are situations where you submit to your wife when it comes to that field because you know she has excellent knowledge in that area of life. Listen to what she says instead of trying to prove a point.

Some men have engaged in certain transactions that have drained them and brought them back to square one, don't be a man that can't listen. Only a good listener can make a good leader, and please respect people with knowledge. It's a lifesaver, don't choose to stay in ignorance because of your Ego or the so-called frame of "I am a man".

Do you notice that A king always has people he consults before taking decisions? He doesn't just take decisions on his own. Do you know that the king is submitting by asking for help in the first place? No man is an island, and I believe that nobody knows it all. Submit to authority, and most of all, submit to God by doing his word; it is in God that you can find meaning in life.

GET A WORK

An idle man is the devil's workshop, if you are inactive, then you will have time to engage in illicit affairs that will destroy you as a man, but when you immerse yourself in work, then you will be productive. The garden of Eden dates back to the creation of the first man Adam; the creator gave him work to do; the first thing to look out for as a man is work and not just work, work in your purpose; purpose defines who you are, purpose makes you attractive, purpose will adorn you as a man, purpose will separate you from all others, you don't just make money, you make it while blessing humanity and also getting fulfilment from it either.

I am a lady, and Purpose makes a queen get attracted to you. I have a guy that was once and is still on my neck. He always comes to me to know how I feel about him; he wants to get intimate with me. I can't date a guy talk less of marrying him when he doesn't know his purpose or lack direction; you are going to be my leader, and the leadership of the house will be entrusted to you, can the blind lead without falling into a ditch?

It's in knowing your purpose that I will be able to be a helpmeet. I remember asking this guy what he wanted to do or where he saw himself in the next 5years from now, and the next thing he told me was that he wanted to travel to the USA, get a green card, build a house, get a car and get married with children. That is success according to society; Success has different definitions for different people. *If you don't understand your definition of success as a man, you will keep using your life to please people, and you will lose yourself at the end of the day.*

It is not about travelling outside the country; *success is not a destination; success is a journey;* it doesn't matter the locality. Stop complaining about your location; some people are doing legit work here and making it big, not the cybercrime many guys are involved in today. I'm talking about real work, not just any job. The money you don't receive as a result of the positive values you've added to the lives of other people will always have wings and fly every time.

It would be best if you dont resort to illegal activities before you make money, don't make a living from making other people cry; for someone to go to that great length to look for money, it means he can wake up and decide to kill someday to make money.

Ritual killing is even very rampant in our world today. As a man, I want you to know that a queen is always interested in your process, not your product, what drives you, not what you drive, who you are, not what you wear. I have asked countless guys how they got to where they are today. There is a story behind the glory, so how did you get to where you are.

I notice something about God. God will always give you two things. There is a place for talent, and there is a place for skill. God will always give you skill with your purpose. Your SKILL is your SAVINGS, while your TALENT stands as your INVESTMENT.

Learn to differentiate between the two because your skill will help you finance your talent. PURPOSE is different from TALENT, your TALENT is your CONTAINER, and your PURPOSE is what you use your CONTAINER to do. You might decide to use a water bottle to pack oil; according to what you have poured into it, the bottle is no longer a water bottle but an oil bottle. If you are good at singing, which area do you want to sing in? Did you want to sing love songs just like Bankyw, or did you want to sing Christian songs just like Mercy Chinwo? Christian songs have a niche, healing songs, grace songs, fuji, e.t.c.

Niche down and be the best in what you do.

A king finds work first, not looking for a companion. Relationship is responsibility; you will buy her a gift on her birthday and vice versa. Love alone can not run a relationship, but that doesn't mean you have to go and get your money illegally. There are many legal ways to make money online, but not until you engage in cybercrime don’t allow a lady to push you into something you will regret later because of love.

A queen wants to help you become a better man.; please never see all ladies as coming to chop your money; *some ladies are tangible assets that you can't just afford to lose; whether they are friends or they are lovers, your life will never remain the same.* Stop chasing slay queens, those that will only slay but with no sense.

In conclusion, *Working on God's purpose makes you successful.* I remembered a day I was on a bike, and this man started complaining about his life, work and how things had been hard for him. As a man, don't start anything without asking God; there is a business that you can do, and not all business goes for you. Why did you think every business people recommended to you ended in futility? Take your time to ask God, not man; there is a business for everyone.

I Was discussing this with my dad the other day, and I started asking him about his process; he told me how he made it. My dad told me he had ventured into different kinds of business before he made it big when he started selling electrical materials. *I understand a secret to life from his story; stop stressing yourself while trying to go your way. The only place you can find the big breakthrough in life is by doing the work God has called you to do.* Have you been in that business for years, but you've always been in debt??? It's about time you ask God exactly what work you're born to do. God gave Adam a job; ask God for the work that will align with your destiny, and you will save yourself from stress and unprofitable hard work.

SELF DEVELOPMENT

Everything in life is a process; without the process, we are not made; clay will only become ceramics by passing through moulding and fire through the hand of the potter. Don't ever rush it. There is a need for Development in every area of life; anything that will stand the test of time has to be built, and growth signifies life.

How valuable you are is embedded in your process; what it takes to build a skyscraper is different from what it takes to build a flat. Your process gives you value; your process determines your durability and effectiveness.

Self-development is continuous throughout life; most people are looking for instant gratification now; I know that there is a lot on men to be financially stable because if you're not a provider as a man, it makes you feel incapacitated. I believe it is not a feeling that only men shoulder but everyone who wants to make meaning out of their life.

Men are raised to bear more responsibility; I understand the oppression in the world today can be overwhelming, but you need to shut your eyes to what is going on around you, your mates that are doing this or your guys that just bought a new car, your temporary status is not permanent, embrace a life of constant learning, it is your process that will make you, continue to push for more.

Development should not be in your financial aspect alone; I have seen men that the only thing they have is money and every other thing needed to keep it isn't there, and this becomes a call for concern when some think about their financial aspects alone without considering other elements. I believe that everything in life works together, if your arms decide not to work today then something would be off, if the eyes says it wants to be alone then it will never have the brain to shelter it, just like if your blood runs and circulate in your stomach alone, every other part of your body will be paralysed.

Life is not just looking for money alone; your mental, emotional, and physical strength also grow along; it is awful when you see the way some guys think even with all their money and qualifications, you need to build character as a man, you need to check your behaviour and build it, you need to care about your physical wellbeing, it is funny when we use our entire youthful days chasing money without taking proper care of our health. It is so saddening that steve jobs, with all the billions in his account, still died of cancer of the pancreas.

Money is not the only essential to living a fulfilling life; at every stage, you are now, please appreciate it, and never allow anyone or anybody to intimidate you. *Just because you do not see results in some areas like others doesn't mean you are not growing.* Self-development is a process that needs to be continuous throughout life.

Maize can take 6months to grow and produce, but a mango can take close to five years to grow and multiply, stop comparing yourself to others. You might be a mango in the making while some can see their result earlier like the maize but which plant has greater strength and root?? The mango. When things seem hard, be more brutal. *Success, as we all know, comes from continuous persistency throughout life.*

Never work on your financial aspect only without working on your mental capabilities; it is a total turn-off when you are a thirty-year-old man thinking like a ten-year-old. A king takes care of other aspects of their life; as a man, you can learn how to cook too, and don't limit yourself to just money mentality; it is attractive to see a man do what other men can't do.

A king stands out from the crowd; he takes proper care of his body; I have a lot of guy friends that sometimes won't bath for two or three days just because they are looking for money, their rooms are scattered, and they only sweep when they have female visitors. Please don't be that kind of man, it is awful when you open your mouth to talk or raise your armpit, and the stench from it can't contain the whole room. Work on your hygiene, and do proper care and maintenance; funny that people in this category will be looking for neat and hygienic ladies.

I believe not all men are in this category but please, if you are the one reading this book right now. Work on that area of your life, *your consistent approach to self-development makes you attractive; you begin to look like what you want to be.* The following are some of the areas I believe you should develop as a man: -

1. Mental building: - Mental building comes from learning, unlearning and relearning; many men don't study areas like marital life and emotional strength; reading will help you achieve much better. I have a guy friend that tells me that he doesn't need books since he is looking for money; you need to build your intellectual capability so that you can contribute your part in meaningful conversations. A queen is intrigued by what you have in your brain more than every other thing; how you think matters a lot to her; from

there, she can determine whether you are the one for her or not when she needs advice on specific issues, she can trust your judgement.

I believe that to even manage money in this time and age; you need knowledge. I run far away from guys that think of money alone in anything they do; I have turned down a lot of guys because of how they think, as a man, you are going to take decisions, you are going to do a lot of things, a queen is turned on when you speak intellectually.

2. Spiritual life: -life is very spiritual, spirituality in the sense that things don't just happen; you need more than the physical to change the world or make it in life. There is a generation of men that thinks spirituality is just for ladies. I have a guy friend Who told me the church is for ladies, and I still wonder how many men still think like that; we have a lot of cubs in lion clothing in the things of the spirit. You can't love a woman right or lead a home without knowing God intimately; I'm not talking about just going to church or looking spooky. Spirituality is internal; it is a lifestyle. Try to know God more intimately today; there are track records of men with great spirituality, and they still made it. Please don't bank on your mother's or wife's prayer; spirituality is personal.... know God for yourself so that fake prophets will not come and prophecy doom into your life; they that know their GOD shall be strong and do exploit.

3. Physical: - A king takes care of himself, there is a reason why I am addressing this issue, but I have to turn this table; a lot of men don't care about how they look; how you look speaks a lot about you, have a good dress sense, work on your hygiene, wash your clothes, please

use deodorant. Oh my God! I remember one time I was on public transport and a guy sat beside me, he was stinking and smiling, he was sweating profusely and the next thing he wanted to get my number, hell no! please work on your hygiene, stop looking rough, iron your cloth, stop sagging too, it doesn't make you look like a responsible man.

4. Leadership: -You don't need to be tall to be a leader; leadership is in the heart, leadership is how well you inspire people, and leadership is being what you want others to be. There is a quote by Mahatma Gandhi that says, "be the change you want the world to be", Every womans want a man that can take charge; I want to look up to you and ask you for help when I need it sometimes. I don't want a man that cries along with me when I need a shoulder to lean on; I want a man that will be there and vice versa. Develop your leadership skills. A perfect place to learn leadership is God's word (the servant leadership); let your life inspire others to be better.

5. Confidence: - confidence is the first ability that makes everyone like you without knowing you; confidence as a man. Every man has Ego but not every man has confidence; please be careful not to be overconfident; it often comes as being arrogant. Be confident in your ability. Know that you are a man before anyone tells you that, you don't need to prove your masculinity to anyone, love yourself, do not settle for anything but the best, give positive energy always, never bring people down but lift them, be bold, and cultivate the skill of courage.

6. Manners: - this one needs to be

addressed; please learn how to approach people, especially a queen. Have you seen how a king approaches a queen? It is with respect and honour. I have seen different men come to me as if they want to do me a favour and I turned them down instantly, one funny guy once told me, he doesn't know why he liked me, there are many ladies?? Who needs all that story? What I have experienced in my life! One met me on the roadside, and the next thing he told me was he wanted to date me; how will you meet someone for the first time and start thinking about marriage. Be a gentleman, take your time to know someone, and I think I am talking from a lady's perspective. You don't just come and impose relationships on people without their consent. Learn how to build friendships and connections with people before making your intentions known.

7. Character:-character makes you stand out from many men; without character, you can never go beyond a particular level in life. Some men are so proud; some men can tell lies; I *remembered a guy who lied to my mum about being a doctor, and he told me he was a lecturer, but he had a passion for plumbing. It's amusing, people; all these lies to get a lady to say yes to your proposal aren't worth it. A* Queen needs to know if you're a man of your words; I prefer truth to a lie because if I later find out you've been playing on my intelligence, then it will hurt me more than not telling me the truth*; it is better not to talk than to lie, be a man of integrity, be a man of your words.* Develop your character intentionally. You will have to restrain yourself from something as a man. Let's be truthful most of our parents endured their marriage, and if you don't want to end up with a

bitter wife, please work on your character. The way you talk to people and interact with people matters a lot. *You can have all the beauty in this world, you can have abs, a manly figure, but without character, you are a disaster waiting to happen.* Your body and packaging are like the icing on the cake, but your character is the actual cake; when I eat icing almost every time, I will surely get sick. Work on being a better man every day for yourself and your queen.

8. Vocabulary building: - I was discussing relationship issues with my best friend, and she mentioned how she hates it when a guy can't construct a complete sentence without committing blunders. The truth is you don't need to have British accents, especially when you are not born in England; just a good command of English will be beneficial to you and, in fact, to your future children. English is a globally recognised language; learn and improve on it.

TEACHABILITY

The happiness of your life, family and the comfort of those around you is based on how teachable you are; if you are not teachable, you will end up hurting the people close to you. When a man is teachable, it makes the work easier because there is a generation of men that is all-knowing, they believe they know it all, and they can't change for anyone.

I recently had a sweet encounter with one of my senior colleagues in my department; he was my assistant supervisor when I was doing my project back then in school. He was putting us through, and he was frustrated at some points and told us we were not serious, and he had been trying to teach us, but we couldn't comprehend his teachings.

He told us we did rubbish after spending close to 5hours on the microscope! I was so mad at him, and I felt like just beating him up; inside my head was smoke of anger rising in me, and I constantly looked at him till he noticed something was wrong with me. I decided not to talk about it to him. He asked me what was wrong, and I said nothing. Inside my head, I was like didn't he know what he did just now? He asked me the second time i was trying to suppress my anger but I couldn't hold it the third time he asked.

I shouted and told him he got me angry, I tried to explain what got me mad. I was doing something for the first time; how did you expect me to get it just like that. I was amazed by his response. He apologised to me and even tried to bribe me with pancakes. The next time I noticed, he was careful not to do it again. He will correct us with love and tell us we are doing well, but we need to put more effort.

Now! that's the man I am talking about, he saw that his words hurt me, and he corrected himself. If you have this trait as a man, trust me, you will have the best marriage on the planet earth, I don't just know how you want to do it, but you will surely get the best smiling wife and the most submissive wive because you care about other people's feelings. You can correct yourself to become a better version for that person.

The reason why some men nurture bitter wives is that they aren't willing to change for anyone in a relationship; they *advocate for the word " this is how I am"*. Some love their girlfriend the way they want to love her, not how she wants to be loved; that is why you keep having problems in your relationship. Love people the way they want to be loved, treat people the way they want to be treated.

Being teachable is a trait that every human being on earth should have; it is the bedrock of non-violent communication; if you're teachable, your social life will be 100%. Teachability helps you see the world from another person's perspective; it saves you against selfishness. *I realise that in life, a word means something different for different people.* You can show a high five sign to someone in America, and he interprets it as "hello", while in an African country, it can be termed as a "curse". Our readings of sentences are different. I might see six, and you will see nine.

A man who can not take correction is called a fool in the book of ancient wisdom; I didn't say that; the wise man that ever lived said it (king Solomon). Teachability can be painful at first for a man. A woman is used to being corrected on different occasions, maybe in the kitchen, manners and e.t.c. The young men are expected to find things out.

Humility and teachability go hand in hand; if you are not humble, you can not be teachable. Understand that as a man, you will always need help in this life because why will God give you parents, siblings, friends, and teachers, if you are meant to know it all as a man.

Please, if you want to have a blissful home and a successful life as a man, you need to be teachable, you need to understand people and come to a junction where you drop your ego for a while, men like that are very scarce, and anything scarce is valuable, and I want you to be part of them, the fact that you are reading this book right now shows that you are a King.

VISIONARY

A man with vision is better than a man with television. I have met a lot of men today who don't even know where they are going in life; some acquire money and spend it on partying, clubbing, drinking, and girls without a vision of where they want to be or even where they are meant to be.

They constantly go along with the tagline "anything comes, and anything goes" having done a little survey of some men that I interviewed personally, I realised that the majority don't even know where they are going. All they care about is getting money, that is why some get 5 million now, and the next thing they think of is getting a car.

I am not moved by what a man drives but by what drives him. I am moved by where he sees himself and his action in accomplishing that task. A *man with vision is better, and I will always choose over a man with money but who lacks direction.* A man with vision has focus and will make a good leader. How will you enter a car that doesn't know where it is going? It is just moving with no destination in view; vision determines the outcome.

It is saddened when you ask some men where they want to be in the next five or ten years, and the only thing that comes to their mind is travelling out of the country or getting a green card. Vision *is something you work towards but can never achieve; you will only be closer to it. Your vision will always outlive you*; for example, if your vision is to see justice in Nigeria, you know you can only reduce injustice but can not curb it entirely.

Do you have a vision board? Have you taken the time to think of where you want to be in the next five years or ten years from now? Instead of some men taking their time to think about their future, they would instead be chasing everything under skirts. *When you are busy with your vision board, you won't have time for irrelevant things. When you are visionary, a queen will notice and acknowledge you.*

Be a man with a vision. Because you are the head and the captain, what happens when the blind leads the blind? They will fall into a ditch. Get a picture of your life first before looking for a companion.

Ask yourself these questions: -

- I'm I in the direction I want to be??
- Are my actions moving me forward to where I want to be or not??
- I'm I willing to pay the price to get there?
- What are the possible more innovative and legal ways to get here?
- Which relationships are irrelevant to where I don't want to be??
- I'm I doing the right thing at this point??

Be honest when answering these questions; I'm not there anyway; it's just you.

Don't be a dreamer, and there was a brother I dated years back when I was still young and naive; he would tell me different fantasies, how he would take me to China and the likes of it. It happened on a particular day. I questioned him, what have you done to make this china dream a reality?? Nothing! You are just talking but no action. *Mouth will not take you to your destination or where you want to be. Talking is cheap, but action is very expensive.*

Don't also be a hard worker without being intelligent and strategic, don't be a jack of all trade master of none; use your time productively in the activities with the highest return.

DON'T BE INTIMIDATED

A king does not make drastic decisions about his life or future because of anyone, whether it is his girlfriend or whatever, he is a man that isn't intimidated or pressured because of someone else's success, and he is comfortable in his strength.

There are a lot of guys engaging in cybercrime today in other to impress ladies or prove a point to people around them. A king is very conscious about how he makes his money because he knows he is a leader, and he should lay a good example.

Don't be intimidated by anybody's wealth so much that it forces you to engage in illegal activities. Everything, consciously and unconsciously, is centred on peace. Aking wants peace in all areas of his life what is the usefulness of money with no peace.

Sometimes I will hear some conversation behind me, some men will start talking about every car on the road, oh! This is benze, this torres, and that and that....... All through and hoping or wishing they have one, I never said you should not desire things like that obviously but don't allow material things to control you, don't allow it dictate how you live your life or be a template through which you judge your success.

There are some men who can only give money but that is the only thing they can give. The wisest king that ever lived said wisdom is a defense, money is a defense but wisdom will keep your life.

the esthers of this generation, the Deborah of this generation doesn't want a beautiful water bottle with no water in it. we are more particular about a guys content than what he can afford because we also don't want to be a liability.

It is easier to criticize the women folk based on the type of girls you've been meeting but you haven't met every single woman, you can't use one experience to judge the entirety of woman, I feel so bad when guys keep telling me that the entirety of women in my generation are looking for money but I will say NO, the real queens I know are looking for more than just money.

Just like some ladies can only offer their body in a relationship some men can only offer money in a relationship, if the only thing you can offer in a relationship is money, then you are not a king. You will mostly attract the hungry ladies, although the concept of attracting who you are, I wont totally agree with it but, the only people that will be attracted to you based on my ideology is those that want your money. *The real queens wont mind telling you NO with all your money.*

Money is not everything, a man of wisdom is better than a man with money but no wisdom, it isn't not worth the investment because he will still go back to being poor, a man of vision is a man of wisdom, the good book says wisdom is better than gold nor silver, don't waste your entire life chasing money let money chase you instead. The more you chase money the more it runs away from you, there is an atmosphere that attracts money to you. Seek wisdom first.

RESPONSIBILITY

A king owns is every decision, he is responsible for any action he takes, he doesn’t try to blame it on anyone or find excuses for himself when things go wrong, I know that the natural instinct of any man both male and female is to run away from responsibilities or try to blame their misfortune on another person, sometimes a man will be caught in illicit affairs and he will blame it on the lady, but you both engaged in it which made you a partaker of something like that

We are in a world that isn’t so balance when it comes to enforcing responsibilities. I noticed that women are taught to be more responsible than men and who else should be more responsible if not the male child. I believe the male child leads and a leader takes responsibility in every aspect. A man should take responsibility for his home, works, decisions, business e.t.c not blaming it on someone else.

Understand that mistakes are inevitable but they can be avoided, own your mistakes and stop giving excuses for it. king David couldn't hold himself accountable for committing adultery with another person's wife. Real men say sorry when they are wrong, it doesn’t make you less of a man.

The past generation of men have this character and I am very curious if it hasn’t been passed on to the next generation of guys that we have today. Indie's father always sees sorry has been weak, he hardly says sorry when he is wrong instead, he tries to blame the situation on circumstances, there is a cultural trait have seen among a lot of guys, they associated "saying sorry to weakness" which shouldn't be.

Saying sorry when you are wrong reflects humility, virtue and most of all responsibility in you, the best way to end a conflict is by saying sorry. Take responsibility for everything you do, don't run away from it.

BE THE KIND YOU WANT

I noticed a lot of men actually has this ideology that virtue is only for the ladies, you are looking for a virgin, are you a virgin? you want someone that is neat and hygienic, are you hygienic?? You want a hard-working woman, are you one yourself??, You want an honest woman but you are full of lies, it's funny how good people end up with bad one's

I recently have some conversation with the guy folks and he expects a woman to keep himself while he cheats around. It isn't meant to be, A king among men doesn't chase everything on skirt, he is that man that has principles and he is willing to go by that principle.

Keeping yourself as a man is doing yourself a favour first. The number of sexual escapades you have as a man doesn't make you more of a man, *somethings have ruined kings and it is not limited to his three things, Adultery/ fornication, drinking and anger.*

I understand that how a man craves for sex is higher than how a woman does but everything in life without proper control will ruin you no matter how little that thing can be, Emotions aren't always right.

Do you even know that it is when you work on that aspect of your life by creating boundaries in that area of life that makes you so unique among men, it doesn't mean you are impotent, there is a natural way to know if you will function as a man and that is the wet dreams you have in the morning, Or the cravings you have

Please sexual purity is not for ladies alone, it is for both genders. Set boundaries on that area of life once you are able to control yourself in that aspect, the devil has lost completely. Sex should only be contained in the container of marriage. It deprives you of your respect as a man when you bring in different shades, some of your men folks will hail you but trust me, the real queens doesn't like that and they distaste it a lot.

BOUNDARIES TO BUILD IN ALL AREAS OF LIFE THAT WILL HELP YOU

✓ Principles For Sexual Purity

- In this world of nudity, it might be hard to keep yourself as a man but you can, just make sure you take your eyes off anything that will contaminate your mind (e.g naked body) whether picture or real life the moment you see it, just take your eyes away from it.
- Don't ever justify any habit, you are the master of your life, so always have the mindset to be better always just because you haven't succeeded in keeping yourself doesn't mean you should accept it as a life style. Whatever you accept you tolerate!
- Don't ever feel pressured in doing something that you don't want to do, don't allow somebody force you out of your will, if the situation requires running, please do.
- Avoid conversations that can trigger such feelings

from you, some words are very toxic to your mind and it can lead you to your vomit.

- Be careful around your female friends, and please define every relationship with every lady unless you are willing to take it to the next level.
- Avoid friends that seems to think having numerous sexual partners is normal, when you move with fools you automatically become part of them.
- Keep conversations open, talk in an open space with a female friend or never be in a position that will trigger sexual feelings in you.

✓ Principles to avoid drinking

- Associate the feelings to pain "Anthony Robbins" in his book "awaking the giant within" said anything you associate pain with has a higher chance of being abandoned, you can always condition yourself to hate drinking by attaching pain to it. E.g., you can start watching documentaries of people that have been affected because of drinking, or the idea of finding yourself in the gutter the next-day could be very embarrassing, this will make you lose your self-respect.
- Let your friends, family know your new commitment so that they can respect your opinion and they won't have to bring drinks for you in a social gathering.
- You need an accountability partner that will be there for you each time you crave to go back to your old ways.
- Avoid scenes that will make you feel drinking is pleasurable and you are missing out.
- Be around people of like-minds so that you won't be forced to try to feel among.
- Replace drinking with something else that is

pleasurable, you might decide to drink a non-alcoholic drink.

- Distract yourself with activities, learn a new skill, take a walk out, go sight seeing and enjoy nature.

 Principles to Control Anger

- Identify the thin line between when you're calm and angry, the breaking point for everyone is different, what is your elastic limit??

- If you have to avoid a scenario that gets you angry then it's better to do that

- Don't talk when you're very angry unless you can suppress it, talk when you're calm and express yourself to the person who offended you.

- Ignore every situation that will get you angry and move on.

- Anger rests in the bosom of fools and if you really respect yourself, you will avoid anger at any cost.

- Listen to music, music is a form of therapy to control any situation, when you're feeling angered

Lastly in every situation prayer works, pray to God about the situation, then you will receive the spiritual strength needed

All these principles will make you stand out among all men, you will not be boycotted by all these bad traits that Ruin great men and even kings. Practice!

BE AN ALL ROUNDER

There is nothing wrong with a guy engaging in domestic activities or helping out in house work, that is why we have a lot of broken marriages today. You don't leave your wife to do all the work .one of my friends once told me he can never enter the kitchen because ladies are meant for the kitchen regardless of the situation. Don't be that kind of Man. It is society that limits every gender to an activity, I was trained up with no gender role, I can put on the generator as a lady, I can carry heavy things the biggest I have tried on my own is a bag of rice. Don't allow the society ideology ruin your home or your future home.

Be good in all things, because when the need arise you won't suffer for it, I was brought up in an independent way. By an independent mother, she can do most things a man can do, she provides too if it is needed. your life will be easier as a man if you stop playing gender roles and just functioning in a particular purpose when need be.

There are many men who can't cook on their own, wash their clothes, take care of their house. They have been brought up to be that way since a woman must do all the house chores. The only thing you have been trained to do is to bring money on the table and watch football. If you are in this category has a man then definitely you need to unlearn it and start cultivating the habit of helping out. that is one of the secrets that will make you have a happy marriage.

Women are helpers not slaves that is why you will see the generation of our fathers, the women are always older because of too much house chores on them, they wash, take care of the children do all kinds of strenuous work and at the end of all these activities they will still have to give sex whether they like it or not. My advice to every man is that if you want a woman to love you and respect you, learn to help out sometimes without her asking you to do so.

A woman multiplies anything you give to her, if you give her a seed she creates a garden for you, give her happiness she multiplies it for you, the peace you all crave for is by helping in the little things although we all feel loved in different ways but no woman will see your heart of kindness and not appreciate you (Queens).

Be selfless if you can get a help just do, to relief her, I am saying this from the perspective of marriage and singlehood, BE AN ALL ROUNDER, stop placing a limit on yourself, if your effort can help anyone now do.

Practice empathy it will help you see the world from another person's perspective, everything mustn't revolve around you.

POLYGAMY SCANDAL

A lot of things has been used to support behaviours that makes men who they are today. According to society it is very weird when we hear that a man is a virgin. In other to prove the promiscuity of a man old conventional ideas says that "men are polygamous in nature".

I have met men who has made this a lifestyle, they think having sex around makes them a GOLDEN MAN, BABA FOR THE GIRLS, I CONQUERED THAT BABE. Some of them see sex as a means of victory, having sex or losing count of your sexual partners is not a king nature.

There is nothing like being polygamous in this case it is the lack of self-control; sexual purity is for both genders. everyone has a polygamous nature both male and female. There was a woman in the bible that had 6 husbands., dont ever belief what the society tell you about sex, you are a king.

A king is not seen around having sex with dogs and cats, Manage your sexuality. I was watching TVC news last two years ago and I heard the story of a particular lady whose mum died at a younger age due to the father's life of fornication. Their mother contacted HIV just because of their father, He died and also killed his wife, he made is family suffer, the daughter who was on live T.V lamented on how hard life was for them. please as a man learn self control, there is something that guarantees your success in life as a man it is the ability to control yourself.

A man who lacks self-control is like a city without a wall, just imagine If joseph has involved in premarital sex with Potiphar's wife, he wouldn't have become the prime minister. Don't allow a day sex to stop you from reaching your destination. *The reason why a lot of men struggle these days is the countless sexual escapades they had.* I met a married man who told me keeping yourself will save you from demonic spirits that might truncate your destiny. You don't know the type of demons or spirit in those people's life, I have heard of people who went from everything to nothing just because they had sex with the wrong people. *Put a zip on that and let it be sacred just for your wife.* As a man if you want to make head ways in life this type of societal conclusion shold be unlearned from your life.

HOW TO MANAGE YOUR SEXUALITY

You might have explored so much that it isn't easy for you to stay celibate on your own, let me give you a quick tip to how to keep yourself for your woman and avoid the trap that fornication or adultery brings to you.

BOUNDARIES: - what are the structures you have put in place that will save you from immorality, sex is not always the problem, what triggers that feeling in you, I don't know you the way you know yourself, but there is something that triggers a feeling in you.

When you can't see in the dark and you need light, the first thing that comes to your mind is going close to the switch to on the light, what triggers the feeling of hunger, an empty stomach, what triggers the feeling of clean teeth, it comes by using a toothpaste.

Sex doesn't just happen, something must have triggered that feeling in you, do you watch pornography videos??, Do you watch erotic movies?? or are you the type of man that is overly careless beside a lady?? You just allow women that you aren't committed to come over to your place without prior notice, they bring food for you and you start eating too. all this thing's keep adding up to your sexual emotions or is it kissing that triggers that reaction in you.

Whatever that is I don't know, you have to figure that out for yourself because that is the reason why you are feeling it.

Once you know that is how you feel when certain things happen then you start putting some rules around it. You might decide as a rule that you don't want female sleep overs, you might decide to stop consuming sexual contents, you might decide to start putting some caution to visiting times.

Doing this as a man will earn you so much respect, you are not being hard you just have boundaries and principles you don't want to compromise on.

IDLENESS: - when boredom sets in, your mind will start playing games with you and you might want to engage in things you have vowed not to do. It is always better to keep yourself busy, it might be reading a book at your free time or learning a course, whatever that is you have to keep yourself from being idle.

I have moved with guys most of the time, I have more guy friends than female friends. But I must tell you that I know that they can start doing somethings when they're bored. There was one of my friends (guy) who use to be very close to me before, he came to my house that day claiming he was bored, I let him in and I can't really remember what transpired that made me to hold his phone and you need to see what he was watching "porn" I was scared for a few seconds and I asked him why he was watching that kind of thing, he only smiled and switch off his phone, that moment I knew he was vulnerable and he needed help, I noticed he stopped talking for some time and their was silence for a while in the room.

I was sensitive enough to understand what was going on in his mind, I told him to let us stroll out for a while and I escorted him to his house because he is just a stone thrown from mine. A minute of idleness can make you do the unthinkable. You need to save yourself from every news flying around, you don't consume everything on social media, most of the contents on social media this day is full of sexual contents. Keep your thoughts because it will direct your life and it starts from not allowing some illicit things fill your mind. If you have to switch off your phone for a while do it, if you have to stroll out for a while do so, whatever you have to do just do, so that boredom will not push you to do what you detest.

Determination: - There is nothing a determined mind can not do; you might say all this thing's I am suggesting isn't easy to do but seriously is there anything in this life that is easy. you have to pay some sacrifice if you want some result in your life, no pain no gain.

Sex will cost you more than you bargained for, remember the pampers you will buy and besides are you old enough to handle fathering a child or even if you're married are you ready to have your family fall apart, what about the STD'S AND STI'S

When you think about the consequences of what you are doing right now then you will be determined not to do it. Just imagine the spiritual implications of it, it is not everybody you should have sex with. I have heard of cases of men who had everything all together, they had the money. The prestige but just a day of vulnerability, a day of sex with the wrong person turned their whole life around. Things began to change for them negatively. Sex is much more than flesh to flesh there is a transaction you are engaging in; I met a married man recently and he told me how is life would have been much better if he had kept himself. He told me he can't count the number of women he had sex with.

He has a reason for what he said, most of you are claiming life is hard but what if it has been that way because of the countless number of partners you've add. Keeping yourself is not a religious thing and it doesn't benefit God in any way but YOU.

Faith: - if you have faith, there is nothing you can't do, you can break unnecessary soul ties you've add with countless number of people through prayer, pray for strength to overcome, and start being intentional about it. You have to work out your faith, when it requires you fleeing or running Especially when the situation is tensed, please do.

All this will help you to manage your sexuality, make a rule today that you will only use your keys to open the door of marriage. Sex outside of marriage will take you further than you bargained for. Some have committed abortion; some have unwanted children out there.

Sex is strong and only marriage can contain it, the pleasure is only for minutes but the regret is for a life time, ZIP IT UP NOW!!!!!!!

HAVE YOUR OWN MIND

I remembered dating a guy who seems to allow his friends control him when making decisions because he believes they know better than him in things of life and looking at his friends, it is written clearly on them that they are not the type he can put his whole life on. But because he is still a boy in a man skin, his friends controlled him even when it comes to our relationship, then I just thought about it one day looking at how his friend's marriage turned out to be... Did you think this people are the best examples to look up to?? Did you want your life to be like theirs?? Are you sure they really know better??

One of his friends brought another woman to his matrimonial home even when the wife was around and had sex with another lady on the matrimonial bed!!!

The wisest man that ever lived said if the blind lead the blind they will both fall into a ditch, if you move with fools in no time, you will start acting like them, and if you move with the wise then you are wise.

Some men can not take decisions on their own, if you can't seat down and think about every advice and counsel before coming to a conclusion then I'm afraid to tell you in a respectful tone that you're still a toddler in a man's clothing.

Have a mind of your own, some men are controlled by their mum, mama's boy that is the popular name for them, before doing anything they first ask for consent from their mum, it's funny when a grown-up man still do that.

I heard of a man who sent the money for their wedding into his mum account instead of his fiancee and told his mum to see to the expenses instead of involving his fiancee, I hope you are not that Kind of man. not having a mind of your own signify that people has a control over your life, they have the key and lock to your life and more like they have a hold to your future.

The worst kind of man to move with is someone who can't think on his own, I am not saying that you shouldn't listen to other people's advice, I am only saying when people say their opinions based on a matters that pertain to your life, take your time to analyse the situation before coming to a conclusion, everyone that advice you might have good intentions but not all good intentions is good for your life.

Not all advices can work for you, don't be so easy to be manipulated by people that they can just decide the outcome of your life, you should be able to make a decision that can suite your life regardless of what anyone thinks about it.

A King has a mind of his own despite the number of advisers that he has, he doesn't take decisions just because others said it, a king looks for the possible best solution to a problem by first analysing and then knowing what exactly he wants.

EMPOWER WOMEN

"Together we rise the better for all of us"

The world is full of competition and I understand that competition is part of life, we have a lot of insecure men out there, there is this old ideology that goes on in almost every man, just because your instinct is to provide doesn't mean others must be below, the world is evolving and we are in a constantly changing world, back in the days the major work available then was farming, our fore fathers will go to the farm while our mothers will take care of the home and children but now we are in the computer age and a lot of things are done professionally, times are changing, before women don't go to school they are only married off before their second monthly period, now women are encouraged to go to school. I believe we have men that isn't insecure about a woman pursuing her purpose, ambition in life.

A woman will always bear your surname and any achievement she has belongs to you. Diming the light of someone in order for you to shine is devilish. but the society will tell you it isn't appropriate. Empower a woman you empower a nation.

I heard a story of a man whose wife used to be a working class before they got married, just because she is receiving a higher pay than the man, the man insist she quits her job and apply for a teaching job of just 10,000Naira per month , later the man died and this woman was left to raise the children on her own on a salary of 10000Naira with three kids, life was so frustrating and miserable for her and the kids she looks 60 @35 all because a man was intimidated by her success.

I know some men already out grown this idea but I still want to emphasize on it , since your woman becomes successful, it is a bonus to you, not a disadvantage and it doesn't make you less of a man, that is why I come to this conclusion that a King amongst men empowers a woman, for a woman to be a better version of herself, confident, more beautiful, well taken care of speaks a lot about who you are, there is no pride in your woman being lower than you.

In a kingdom a queen can rule just like a king when you are not around. If your queen doesn't represent who you are, then you just failed. They say by their fruit we shall know them, the depth of your riches, intellect, prowess should be seen in your Queen.

Let your woman be able to stand beside you, a queen will never be attracted to a man that will be intimidated by her success, she wants a man that will groom her and prune her to be the best, one of the greatest leaders in Hebrews in the old century said that any kingdom that divides against itself will not stand.

A king and a queen both own kingdom, when there is constant strive then nothing good will come out of it. It is partnership not competition, it is Oneness not division.

Men are transactional and because they are. They tend to do something based on what they will gain from it. I have met some men that always either want to lay with you just in a bid to help you. If you have the capacity to help a woman, please do it. Help without asking for anything in return. The only person that can reward you is God.

WHY SHE SAID NO

Most men equate everything to money, a queen can reject you with all your physical possession because she is interested in who you are, stop trying to impress anyone. Below are some of the reasons she said No: -

Lack of direction: - A queen will never elope with a man that has no vision, goals or dreams, have you met men that just live life like they will die tomorrow this popular song in Yoruba "ma Jaye Ori mi, mi o Meyin Ola" translated to "I will live my life like I want it, I'm not thinking of my future". we start living now!! Let me ask you a question, if you were asked to enter a car that has no destination in view would you have entered that car??, I know exactly what your answers will be "NO". why will you try to ask a person out especially a queen for that matter when you don't even know where you are going. First set your priorities right first, know where you are going and don't put somebody into your confusion.

Manner of Approach: -The way you approach a lady is very important, some men will just meet you on the way and talk to you like their fellow men, imagine someone walking up to you for the first time and telling you they want to date you, or they will tell you, you are very lucky that they are approaching you, talk to her with a respectful tone. stop being arrogant, use words like if you don't mind can I have your number?, have a good sense of humour, compliment her hair or dressing or beauty. You can always tell her it will be lovely if I can be friends with this beautiful lady, be soft and gentle in your approach.

Hygiene: - I remembered a day in my life that was when I was very young, just in my teenage year then, a guy with a dirty boxers approached me, how did I know his boxers is very dirty, imagine sagging with a dirty boxers, it was a total turn off for me, everything he said was entering and coming out of my right ear. i was disgusted by it. Not only your clothes alone, take care of your body, I have seen a lot when it comes to guys, I have friends that don't even take their bath for three days, there was a guy who use to be my neighbour during my undergraduate days in the university, he only sweeps his room when someone comes visiting, whenever he is sweeping we know that he has a visitor, some men merely by opening their teeth, the whole room won't be able to contain it, they have different shades of colour on their teeth. Take care of yourself, erase the old mentality of who I'm I trying to impress?? I only need to make this money; I don't need to take care of my body.

Dishonesty:- I met a guy who told my mum he was a doctor, he didn't know my mum already told me about him, then he told me he was a lecturer in open University and he teaches computer science, *interesting I wanted to ask him questions on computer science imagine what a so called lecturer said, he said computer science is the act of cyber cafe,* the reason why I use this guy is because he is one of the most untruthful person I have ever met in my life, so I still remember him vividly. Please be honest about who you are, the fact that you painted a false personality doesn't mean you can impress a queen, Queens fall in love with who you are, sincerity. Even if you have cars of different colours anyone that will reject you, will.

Values not aligning: - can two walks together except they agree, one of the main reasons could be because you don't have things that govern your life, you don't really have the same values on relationship or life in general, she might love things to go a certain way but you don't want it that way there is already a clash, your purpose might be different in a way that it is entirely opposite from hers. She might have a certain belief about relationship and what she wants but you don't think on that direction. For example, she will like to wait till marriage before having sex.

Bad character: - some men are very rude not only to ladies but even to other people around them. Most times you might try to hide your bad character from a lady because you're interested in a queen your bad character can be noticed through how you treat other people around them. Work on your character! Don't accept it!!

QUALITIES OF A QUEEN AND HOW TO IDENTIFY THEM.

I have an online community where I talk to men and most men complain about not meeting the good ladies, I will share with you how you can identify one down below, these are some qualities that signifies a real queen: -

Builder:- A queen is driven about the future not just the present, she is constantly building and learning, she is constantly trying to be better in everything she does, she isn't a mediocre, she is looking for someone who isn't comfortable with stagnancy but someone who can dream big, most times insecure men, clowns, frogs are always intimidated by her because she is what they don't have, she can see beyond the physical, she can determine whether you're a good investment, she is looking for a partner not a competitor, she is looking for an angel not a devil.

Multiplier: - there is a lot of old conventional ideas that men have about a lady. They see them as a liability. A dumb person, a damsel in distress looking for who to help her, she is seen as someone who sucks away your money, or your progress, some men are scared of revealing their account to their wives because they are scared, she will keep demanding for so much until it finish. A queen is a multiplier, anything that comes into her hand multiply geometrically she is constantly chastising you for spending recklessly, she is your manager, you can always trust her with your money or other valuables, she is worth more than rubies because She is full of wisdom, knowledge and understanding, she understands the world of business, she is a learner. She knows how to invest. The moment you meet her, she exposes every area of your life that you never even know you have.

Intelligent: - it takes a real king to face a real queen, when she begins to question you, you had better get ready for her answers, she is not meant for every man, that is why the only person that can compliment her is a king of a man. Everything about her speaks about, beauty, class and dignity. She is a force to reckon with anywhere she goes; she is not just an epitome of beauty but an epitome of knowledge, men respect her intelligence. She is someone who hates ignorance, she is a constant reader, everything that comes out of her mouth is full of wisdom, when a queen talks, you suddenly develop goose bumps, all men adore her, she chooses, she isn't desperate because she knows how valuable she is ...her appearance commands respect.

Silent energy: - A queen doesn't talk much, she has a silent energy that can't be compared to any other woman, her quietness speaks of confidence, high self esteem and a lovable spirit, she is an observer and won't unwrap herself on a first date. She is every man's dream.

Purpose driven:- A queen knows she is meant for more, she knows that she is not a baby factory nor does her office resides only in the kitchen, she looks beyond and can see where she is going, she has a vision and a purpose she is pursuing and she is very keen on achieving it, she doesn't care what others think about her but she is busy pursuing what she is called to do on earth, her purpose defines her and she is looking for a king that aligns with her purpose, she is a busy person and you should be lucky if you are able to get her attention, her time means a lot to her and she doesn't give it to just anyone. She is the woman who knows her core value and reason for her existence.

Principles: - A queen lives a very disciplined life, she has principles guiding her life, when you see her, you will surely know that she is different, she had rules guiding her decision, she takes into consideration every decision before doing it. She is the woman who seems to have a hold of her life, merely seeing this attracts you towards her. She is a woman who will never compromise her standard for anyone, she isn't easy to persuade, she knows what she wants out of life and in order for her to achieve it, she has built a set of rules around her life. Show me a woman who is purposeful and successful, I will tell you she lived a principled life.

Honesty: - A queen is very truthful; she is the woman that you can trust with your life. She lived an honest life with everyone around her, she believe there is nothing good that can come out of a lie, she demands the same from everyone, the best way to get on her nerves is if you are not truthful, live an honest life today.

God fearing: - charm can be deceiving and beauty fades away but a woman who Honor's the Lord deserves to be praised. A queen loves God passionately and she is willing to do just anything to please God and she demands the same from anyone she will like to spend the rest of her life with. You can always put your confidence in her because her every decision is guided by the word of God.

Self control: - A Queen has self control you can always trust her with your life, she is a virtuous woman in and out, she is emotionally mature, she knows how to handle situations maturely, she runs away from strife, anger and fornication. She can control herself in every situation. She has a balance to life.

Teachable: -She embraces correction because she knows that no one knows it all, she listens to instructions and intentionally acts on it. A woman who is teachable is meek and gentle. But when correcting a queen, it is always good to tune down your voice, it's a sign of respect.

Irresistible: - She is a woman you can always be vulnerable around; she will never take your love for granted but she will reciprocate with the same energy, she is a woman who has her own thing, she will make you a proud man that even your friends will wish she was theirs. When you see this trait in your woman, don't let her go. Who can find a virtuous woman for her prize is far above rubies?

Chooses her cycle: - A lot of people want to be her friend but she chooses her association wisely, she is friendly to all but she has a small cycle of loyal friend or friends. She moves with people of like minds.

How To Know if she loves you: -

- Helps you achieve your goals and vision: - She is concerned about your dream, a queen has a love nature, that is who she is, she isn't selfish she is concerned about your life, dreams, goals, vision. She wants you to be more when she comes into your life, she sees it has a goal to make sure you reach your potential.
- Good motivator: - She uses her word to stir you up, you are always motivated to go the extra miles, is life not great when someone believes so much in you and motivate you to reach your potential.

When she truly loves you regardless of your financial status in thick or thin, she will surely be your greatest cheer leader, she is loyal to you regardless of the circumstances.

- Get to know who you really are: - She is interested in you not in your car, house, she wants to know your funny side, vulnerable side regardless, what makes you happy or sad?? Who your parents are, your family? Your best food. She is interested in your details.
- she is a good counsellor: - She not only motivates but counsels you, when she sees an opportunity, she instantly talks you into it. She advises you and keep reminding you of your commitments, your life automatically become hers and she will push you with her words to your greatness.
- She chooses the part of purity: - She keeps herself for you, she is virtuous and chooses to honour you by keeping herself. She won't start having sex with every man all around but she is waiting for the right container which is marriage to have sex with you. A queen values purity, it is her life style.
- She is committed to you: - The worst woman you can ever toast is a woman who is in love, a queen doesn't date every dick and Harry, she dates with a purpose and a future in view one reason why she chooses commitment. The woman who loves you will be committed to you.
- She will introduce you to important people in her life: - Beware of secret relationships, if she tells you she doesn't want anybody to know then you are not the one, a lady who really loves you is looking forward to introducing you to her siblings, friend's, family e.t.c.

MINDSET OF A KING THAT WILL MAKE HIM PROSPER IN ALL THINGS.

Everything I have written will surely transform you, I want to tell you about the wisest man on earth, who finished from the university of wisdom, he has over 3000 proverbs to his name and a thousand song. His name is king Solomon, being a King, he has countless experiences and he has also made some mistakes in his life that has led him astray, here is his advice for the king's.

According to one of his proverbs, He talked about King Lemuel's mothers advise.

Proverbs31:3

Don't spend all your energy on sex and all your money on women; they have destroyed king's

Sex: - sex is very sacred that it should only be in the confines of marriage, because everyone engage in it outside marriage doesn't make it normal. The society we live in has normalised promiscuity for men but to stand the test of time you need to keep yourself for the right woman, sex can drain you of your energy.

Women:- imagine a woman talking to you about her kinds, he knows the depth at which having too many women in your life can bring you down in life, not all women are queens, some are just there to drain you of your money, privileges and suck you dry(Samson and Delilah) that is why you don't spend your money on women, find the right woman (queen) and spoil her.Your money is for your wife, you can be generous to others but don't overdo it, you can all testify that if everything has been tried to capture a man what will always capture a man is a woman so make sure you're with the right one.

Proverbs31:4-7

"Listen, Lemuel. Kings should not drink wine or have a craving for alcohol.........................."

Alcohol: - The society will tell you has a man that the more you drink, the more of a man you become, no wonder a lot of men have been enslaved into that mentality, now a lot of men compete with themselves in beer parlours, clubs on who can take more alcohol than another. Alcohol is for people who are depressed, at the point of death, poor, it is for those who are in misery they drink it to forget their unhappiness and poverty. A king shouldn't be seen with just a cup of it.

Proverbs 31:8-9

> *"Speak up for people who can not speak for themselves, protect the rights of all who are helpless..................."*

Protection: - A king of a man protects, one of the reason God created you apart from being a provider is to be a protector, Be the mouth piece for helpless people, be generously caring to people around you. Don't be stone hearted. Love people when they are facing hard times be there for them. A lot of men nowadays are selfish, don't help people because you are expecting something in return, help people with no expectations from them, yet speak the truth. Be a different man, speak against injustice in your country or society. The way you treat others around you is the way you will surely treat people close to you.

Put everything in this book to practice and you will become so irresistible to a lot of people. Welcome to the uncommon yet Normal, you just unlocked the hidden potential to becoming a great man.

ACKNOWLEDGEMENT

I sincerely appreciate all my stakeholders worldwide (*Dunsin Oba Nigeria, kirubel kitaw Ethiopia, Kiplagat Lawrence Kenya, Raphael Folorunsho Nigeria, Janet Quansah Ghana, Mrs Iletutu).* Thank you for believing in my dreams and vision; you are the best.

I will like to specially appreciate my parents(*Mr and Mrs Ogunbunmi)* for their support financially towards the release of this book, most especially my mum.

Lastly, I want to appreciate myself for all the sleepless nights, the hard work, and the prayers to put this master's piece together. I desire that this book gets to the hand of every man out there.

BOOKS BY THIS AUTHOR

Guard Your Heart

Love is beautiful when you are with the right person, GUARD YOUR HEART is for every single ladies who wants to give their heart to the person who is worth the wait!

you dont need to date every dick and harry before meeting your prince, it is a book that helps you keep your emotions in check so that you can clearly give your love to the right person.
After studying myself and emotions for five years , I finally figured out how to tame it and keep it in check, your emotions are your weakest point as a lady, it could break or make you one reason why you need to guard it for the right Man.

you will be learning the following things at the end of reading this book
1. How to keep your emotions in check
2. How to know a mans intention before dating him
3. how to identify the right prince
4. Qualities you should watch out for when picking
5. self-development before meeting him

Enough of being vulnerable around those that will take you for granted . GRAB YOUR COPY NOW!!!!!!

www.ingramcontent.com/pod-product-compliance
Lightning Source LLC
LaVergne TN
LVHW050341160826
845677LV00014B/3718